Contents

I0202319

Dedication

Psalm 118: 17-19

I will not die but live, and will proclaim what the Lord Has done. The Lord has chastened me severely, but he has not given me over to death. Open for me the gates of the righteous.

I would like to dedicate this book to my dear mother, Carrie Green, my father Lonnie Ferguson and my oldest brother Johnnie Green. My mother and Johnnie both died of cancer. I am also dedicating this book to my oldest sister Lula Mae Dyson and my beloved brother, Richard Earl Green Sr. who are both deceased as well. Lula Mae inspired me and showed me that I could survive this journey because she was a cancer survivor of 22 years. Richard, my youngest brother, was like a son to me. During his final stages of dementia, my battle with breast cancer was just beginning. He did not know I was diagnosed with cancer.

The love for all of you will always remain in my heart.

Acknowledgements

To my husband, Elder Rollin Cleveland, of 40 years, thank you for being the most dedicated person throughout this entire ordeal. To my beautiful children, Ronald, Leona and Shekelia, who took time out of their busy schedules to make sure my needs were met. To my twin brother, Jackey Green, thank you for your love and support.

To my Pastor Overseer, Jeanette Harley and my church family who spent dedicated times with me in prayer and supplication. (Phillipians 4:6,7)

To my special church sisters, Michelle Brown and Yvette Bryant, who took me to my out of town doctor appointments.

To three special sisters, Yvonne Singleton, Juanita Thomas, and Pamela Coaxum. A special cousin, Rose Marie Green, who always called and visited me during my chemo treatments. To my oncologist, Dr. Newberry and my radiologist, Dr. McNabb, who never gave up on me.

A special thank you to all of my relatives, in-laws, friends, neighbors and medical staff. I thank God for all of you!

Chapter One

My Life with God and the Church before Cancer

The love for God and the church became my passion. I wanted to grow in grace and the knowledge of HIM. There were many circumstances and obstacles I had to overcome. Now thirty-two years later, after giving my life to God, he has kept me. I thank God for his grace, his mercy and overwhelming love for me.

My true spiritual foundation was laid under the leadership of Elder Willie J. Fennell, at the Oaks True Holiness Church. This is where my spiritual walk began as a result, my love and devotion for God has grown tremendously.

I am currently worshiping at the Family Worship Center, where the Pastor is Overseer Jeannette Harley. I truly thank God for the two churches and the saints. They encouraged me, prayed for me and showed me much love. Words cannot express the gratitude that I have for them.

I now live my life for Christ, in the fullness of God. The enemy knows that I am devoted to live for God so he attacked my body but the one thing that I do know is that I have the victory in Him. Psalm 1:3 tells us, he shall be like a tree planted by the rivers of water that cannot be moved.

I was saved and living for Christ fifteen years without my husband being saved. After fifteen years of continuing on my mission, to live a life devoted to serving God, my husband finally gave his life to the Lord. He is now an ordained Elder of the church, preaching and teaching the word of God.

It is so important to be the example for your family members and others that you come in contact with. They have no choice but to see the light that shines within you. I Corinthians 7:14 tells us that the unbelieving husband is sanctified by the wife and the unbelieving wife is sanctified by the husband.

I thank God for choosing me. He called me out of darkness into the marvelous light. I will never cease to give Him praise and glory for all he has done for me.

Chapter 2

The Journey Begins

I was lying on my bed one night doing my monthly breast exam, to my surprise I found a lump in my right breast. I immediately called and scheduled an appointment at the Women's Center in Beaufort. I went in for a mammogram and the mammogram confirmed that there was indeed a lump in my breast. My surgeon ordered more testing; an ultrasound, x-rays and a biopsy. After the tests were completed, I had to wait on the results. I had to go through the weekend waiting and praying about the outcome of the tests.

On Monday morning, as I sat on my couch, the phone rang, it was the call my family and I had been waiting on; the call that could change the rest of my life. When I answered the phone, the voice on the other end of the phone confirmed my deepest fears. I was told that I have stage three cancer in my right breast. I was also told that the cancer had already spread to the lymph nodes under my arm. With this devastating news, it seemed as if life for me and my family was on a downward spiral. All of this took place on October 22, 2013. A day I will never forget.

There was another test ordered, a PET scan, to see if the

cancer had spread to any other part of my body. Thank God, it did not. There was also another exam scheduled to see if I was a gene carrier. That test was also negative but they did find another lymph node that was sitting outside of my lungs.

At this point, I was at stage four cancer and the lymph nodes needed to be removed. My oncologist began looking for a specialist that would be able to do the surgery. Thank God he found a reputable surgeon to perform the surgery. The lymph nodes were removed from my lungs and the surgery was a success. Thankfully, the lymph nodes were not cancerous. Therefore, instead of being at stage four I was back at stage three.

My doctor told me that things were so bad that the outcome did not look good for me. I was given a span of two years to live. All this information was given to me and my family before the final pathology report was in. I then had many questionable thoughts about my life. However, I didn't have any questions about my faith.

The cancer was in my body but not in my spirit! I know without a shadow of a doubt that the God I serve is a healer. God told me through his word that I shall live and not die. He said my faith shall make me whole. This ordeal has taken my faith to another level. At this point in my life, nothing can shake my faith!

Chapter Three

The Path of Chemotherapy

I was told during my consultation with my surgeon that I was diagnosed with a very rare form of cancer. I was also told that this type of cancer is rarely found in black women. It is called Triple Negative Metastasis Carcinoma. This rare form of cancer would not respond to regular treatment. It had to be attacked aggressively. It had to be attacked head on with radical chemotherapy to destroy the cancer cells.

So with this report, my family took me to Charleston, South Carolina to see a specialist at the Hollings Cancer Center. There, I met with Dr. Herman. I was given an appointment to meet with her at her office in Bluffton, South Carolina to further discuss my treatment plan. At my appointment in Bluffton, Dr. Herman informed me that I had to start my chemo right away. Therefore, I was scheduled for surgery immediately to put in a port a cath. The surgery was performed at Hilton Head Hospital in December 2014. After the surgery, I had to wait seven days before I could start my chemo treatment. I went to see my oncologist for the dates that I would have chemotherapy. I was told that I had to have chemo for six months; every 21days.

The Journey of a Cancer Survivor

After the 3rd round of chemo, the oncologist ordered an ultra sound to determine if the mass and lymph nodes had shrunk. Two days later he received the report from the radiologist. The results were promising. It showed what he was looking for at that point of my treatment. The chemo treatment was working. It was killing the cancerous cells in my breast and the lymph nodes.   My doctor was very pleased with the results.

I thanked God for the miracle he was performing in my body. I can say that his grace and mercy was the key to my healing. My faith, my beliefs and my love for him will never cease. Thirty-two years ago I answered the heavenly call on my life and from that day I knew that I could go through anything with the Lord on my side.

After the final round of chemo I had a Lumpectomy. This procedure also removed the lymph node from my breast and under arm so that in years to come the cancer will not return. I was told that I would need to have radiation to kill any mass that was left after the surgery. The things that I endured from chemotherapy and the changes that occurred in my body were very devastating.   I lost my hair, I had no appetite, my face had burn spots on it, my skin was so dry, my tongue had dark spots on it and my finger nails and toe nails were black.

During the third round of chemo I went to see my doctor to check my blood count. The count was very low. The number was not what the doctor expected. As a result, my temperature was high and my body was full of fevers. I had to go in the hospital because I needed a blood transfusion. While in the hospital, I was told that I now have strep throat. Therefore, my body is yet again fighting another attack. I was given some antibiotics for my strep throat.

I had been fighting chemo for six months. After every round of chemo there were shots I had to get that helped build up my immune system; my red blood cells, white blood cells and my bone marrow because the chemo kills it all.

HEBREW 11:1

NOW FAITH IS THE SUBSTANCE OF THINGS HOPED FOR AND THE EVIDENCE OF THINGS NOT SEEN.

Chapter Four

The Journey Doubles

This is where the journey doubles. After being diagnosed with stage three cancer in October 2013, my husband was diagnosed in November of the same year with prostate cancer. Approximately one year earlier he had his Prostate-Specific Antigen (PSA) checked. At that time it was very high, therefore he had to have a biopsy done immediately. After having that done, his PSA was even higher than it was before.

So now he had to see the oncologist. My husband was diagnosed with stage three cancer, so now the topic of discussion was surgery. He had to have his prostate removed. He was told that once it was removed there would be no more cancer left in his body. He had the surgery on April 6th of that year causing him to be out of work for six weeks. My husband did not have to have chemo nor radiation. He was completely healed of all the cancer. We just thank God that it did not spread to any other parts of his body.

Six weeks later he went in for his follow up appointment to receive his final pathologist report. He was free of cancer.

All I can say is "God is an Awesome God!" He can do all things but fail. I know that God has a way of getting our attention. I know that he has a reason for everything that we go through. My husband and I have a testimony that will be a blessing to others. I thanked God that my husband was totally cancer free but my fight was not over.

After my fourth round of chemo, I got really sick. I was hospitalized again with a high fever. There were a lot of tests performed to determine what was going on in my body. After a while, I received the results. The doctor stated that all of my vital numbers were very low and that I would need to have a blood transfusion to help the numbers come back up. There was another problem that occurred. They found out that the chemo that I was getting was too strong. So they decided to reduce the amount to see if that was causing my blood count to drop. I had one more treatment left, but my doctor told me that he was going to stop me from getting it. On April 16, 2014 he ordered an MRI to determine if the chemo had killed the cancer cells. The result of the MRI showed that I was cancer free. **To God be the Glory for all that He has done!**

ISAIAH 53: 4-5

SURELY HE HATH BORNE OUR GRIEF AND CARRIED OUR SORROWS: YET WE ESTEEM HIM STRICKEN SMITTEN BY GOD AND AFFLICTED, BUT HE WAS WOUNDED FOR OUR TRANSGRESSION HE WAS BRUISED FOR OUR INIQUITIES. THE CHASTISEMENT OF OUR PEACE WAS UPON HIM AND BY HIS STRIPES WE ARE HEALED.

Chapter Five

The Journey Continues

I didn't know what to expect beyond this point but I knew that everything would come together. Now the unknown of how radiation would affect my body was before me. I knew that God can and would take care of me through this ordeal. The enemy tried to bring doubt to my mind but I thank God that I can resist him because I know that when God does something it is finished.

I just couldn't imagine going through what I went through without my children. The news was very devastating to them. Their mother and father were both diagnosed with cancer. My son would drive for miles to be with me for all of my doctor appointments and all three of my surgeries.

Chapter Six

Final Destination (God is a Healer)

I begin this chapter with a scheduled consultation with my surgeon, Dr. Herman. The consultation was on May15, 2014 to discuss my upcoming surgery. She gave me some very promising news. This "cancer" that tried to take over my body for seven months is no match for the God that I serve.

I thank God for a complete turnaround. My surgery was scheduled on May 21, 2014. Thank God the surgery was a success and all went well with no complications.

The next phase was the life of radiation for the next six weeks to stop any chance of the cancer returning. The final pathology report confirmed that no cancer was found. Dr. Herman stated that, "YOU ARE CANCER FREE."

The reality of this disease could cause one to lose focus because there are so many emotions that come with such a battle. This disease tried to take over my life but God has given me another chance. I have a new outlook on life. I appreciate every moment the Lord has given me. Even though I had some weary moments I never thought about giving up. Quitting the race was never an option for me. I kept myself motivated as I stood on God's word. I am so thankful to God for every blessing he has given me. For every person he placed in my life during this journey. I must praise God because I know that he has a divine destiny for me. Through it all I am a survivor. I give God thanks for each passing day that he gives me here on earth. It surely is a wonderful gift that makes me appreciate my life even more.

I had to have radiation from July 22, 2014 thru September 16, 2014. Thank the Lord I made it!!!

Now I am on the road to recovery but before the healing begins, here comes another obstacle on the horizon. The lymph nodes that were removed from under my arm caused me to swell around that area. I had to see my doctor and he said I was developing lymphedema. When you have so many lymph nodes removed it causes you to swell. I lost range of motion in my arm. Therefore, it was very painful to use it. One can only imagine the pain that I was going through. I had to have four weeks of physical therapy in order to use my arm. For the God I serve is more than able to see me through. He will not put more on you than you can bear. Now that I am on the road to recovery and free from cancer, my soul purpose is to continue giving God the praise and glory for the rest of my life.

I give thanks for my beautiful and loving family. I thank God for those that took the time to be with me during my doctor's visits and all my chemo treatments. I had a great support system and words can't explain how much I appreciate them along with my Pastor Jeannette Harley, my dear sisters Michelle Brown and Yvette Bryant. They also traveled with me to my many doctor appointments. Their love and support will always be with me along with my church family who pushed me in prayer and well wishes.

I JOHN 4:7

BELOVED LET US LOVE ONE ANOTHER FOR LOVE IS OF GOD: AND EVERY ONE THAT LOVETH IS BORN OF GOD AND KNOWETH GOD: FOR GOD IS LOVE.

Chapter Seven

Life after the Cure

Now the mental hurdle begins; not only for me but for my loving husband as well. Unless you have been diagnosed with cancer, it is hard to imagine the battles I endured to get me where I am today.

There were many challenges after the cure. There were mental, physical and spiritual battles that came along with the cure. There are scars that I have to look at daily and they are constant reminders of what I had to overcome. I would have never thought that my body would be attacked so aggressively but life after the cure is a constant reminder of how good my God is.

This ordeal has created an even stronger bond between my family and I. We treasure each moment that we have together and we make sure that the love we share for each other is expressed constantly.

The cure was not just for me but for my family as well.

Chapter Eight

From the Eyes of my Family

"The Day Everything Changed for me."

When my mom was diagnosed with breast cancer, ironically it was 40 years to the day in which I was born. As the oldest of my mother's children, I felt the weight of the world upon my shoulders. I work in the healthcare field so I started researching this highly aggressive form of breast cancer. When we were informed that my mother had stage three cancer, it was quite the rollercoaster ride. I can say that through this ordeal my mother and father never blamed God for this disease. We know that God is love. How thankful we are to know that both my parents have been declared FREE OF CANCER.

Ronald Cleveland

I remember my mother telling me the things I needed to know as I was growing up. We had many conversations about her expectations for my life. She wanted me to avoid making the same mistakes she made.

One of the things she would tell me is that she did not want me to have children before I was married. She didn't want me to go through some of the things she had to go through. I did have a child out of wedlock but a year later I got married and out of that union, four babies were born. We also have an adopted son. We welcomed him to the Cleveland family with lots of love because all children are a gift from God.

When my mother told me she was diagnosed with cancer it really took me to an unexplainable level in my life. I lived with my mother so I witnessed the many sleepless nights. If she could not sleep, I could not sleep. I tried my best to make sure that all of her needs were met.

Mom did not have an appetite so I had to make sure that she would eat enough to maintain her physical strength.

I saw my mom take on this battle like a champ, with no complaints. She never shed a tear during this ordeal. My mother Joyce Green Cleveland is a phenomenal woman of God with great faith.

Leona Cleveland

I could remember just as clear as day in October 2013 when my mother called me to tell me that she was diagnosed with cancer. Not only was there a diagnosis but the doctor gave her two years to live. At first, I was shocked and could not believe this was happening. I must admit that there were days and nights that I did cry. I heard about cancer my entire life but to actually have it affect someone so close to me, was just devastating.

Approximately one month later my father was also diagnosed with cancer. At this point I felt as if I was having a nightmare. The only thing that I wanted to do was wake up from this crazy dream, but then I realized that this was a reality.

At this point, all I could do was pray. Initially, I told the Lord that I really did not understand why I was going through this season in my life but then I was quickly reminded of the hymn which states, "Whatever My Lot, Though Has Taught me to Say, It is Well!"

I began to give God thanks in spite of what was going on all around me. Through the many doctor appointments, surgeries, chemotherapy, blood transfusions, radiation, and hospitalizations, I stood on the word of God, knowing that he was going to heal my parents. If anything, this experience has proven that the Lord is strong and mighty and he is definitely mighty in battle.

I want to take this opportunity to thank my parents for their undying faith in God, especially my mother, who never shed a tear throughout this entire process. It was truly remarkable and pleasant to witness.

As a result of this season, my relationship with the Lord has grown to another level and I trust him more now than I did two years ago. In the words of Kurt Carr, "There's no doubt, my God can't do the impossible; I know he can because I've seen him do it. He can turn that mess you're in, into an awesome miracle; I know he can because I've seen him do it."

I stand here today in 2015, to declare that both my parents are healed from cancer. "There is Nothing My God Cannot Do!"

Shekelia Joyner

The Journey of a Cancer Survivor

My aunt Joyce is a woman of Integrity, a woman who stood on faith alone and very submissive to what God had in store for her. Not one time did she question why she had to endure the obstacles that stood in front of her, instead she moved slowly into the contraction zone. God had some work to do!

These road blocks were just that, road blocks. God knew what path she was going to take prior to her approaching the work zone. God had her find the knot in her breast and began to prepare her for the work ahead. When I received the news that my aunt had breast cancer, it felt as if I was being squeezed, losing all juice. I said to myself, " I've been here before, losing my dad to cancer! I knew the road ahead would be a rocky one!" I just couldn't understand how this cancer came about. I wanted to just curl up in a little ball and cry. I could hear my aunt on the other end of the phone telling me not to cry because she was going to be fine. How did she know this? It was one of the hardest things I had to deal with, but it was merely a small construction zone in which I needed to move slowly through. I knew in the end we would be back to speed.

When I would see her after chemotherapy or just coming by for her medications, she always had a look of determination! She was never afraid of this disease because she knew she didn't have to fight it alone. Never once did I see her shed a tear. What a strong woman she is! God opened up a new road for her to proceed with caution on her way to recovery.

Today and every day I just thank God for allowing her to be with us longer! "The Shepard always takes care of his Sheep's"

Love you Auntie

Natasha aka "tashie" "Cinderella"

About The Author

Joyce G. Cleveland is a native of St. Helena Island, South Carolina. She attended Beaufort High School until the 10th grade because of circumstances that were beyond her control. In 1975, she married Rollin Cleveland. They had three children, Ronald, Leona, and Shekelia. Joyce worked in manufacturing for 12 years. She worked in the food service industry for 32 years. For five years she was an entrepreneur and owned her own restaurant, "Joyce's Home Cooked Meals". Cooking is her passion.

Joyce previously attended Oaks True Holiness Church for 22 years. She currently worships at Family Worship Center and has been there for six years.

Joyce is the prospective cancer survivor spokesperson for the Health and Wellness Department at the Family Worship Center. She enjoys working with the Youth Pastor as a chaperone with the youth and serving under great leadership.

www.ingramcontent.com/pod-product-compliance
Lightning Source LLC
Chambersburg PA
CBHW051051030426
42339CB00006B/310